KNOSSOS

© ADAM EDITIONS 275, MESSOGION AVE., 152 31 ATHENS
TEL.: (01) 6721801-3, 6470072, TLX: 214223 ADAM GR, FAX: (01) 6725015

KNOSSOS

MYTHOLOGY-HISTORY
GUIDE TO THE ARCHAEOLOGICAL SITE

ANTONIS VASSILAKIS

ΕΚΔΟΣΕΙΣ ADAM EDITIONS

Editor: Costas Adam
Editing of texts: Kiki Birtaha

Translation: Daphne Kapsambelis
Photographs: Yiannis Yiannelos, Costas Adam, Archaeological Receipts Fund
Reconstructions : Kostas Iliakis
Layout : Thodoris Anagnostopoulos - Thymios Presvytis

TABLE OF CONTENTS

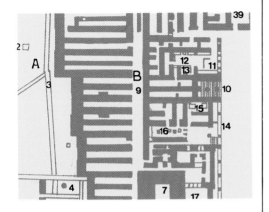

HOW TO USE THIS GUIDE

The following symbols have been used on the maps and plans which accompany the text:

- The capital letters **A** - **S** define the functional units of the palace and the most important buildings around it.

- The numbers **1** - **48** identify the most important rooms or areas of the palace and of the houses that are nearest to it.

Most of the names of the various areas were established by the archaeologist, Sir Arthur Evans and are conventional, not always corresponding to their actual function. However, they have been used here for the sake of consistency with other texts and with the indicative signs within the archaeological site.

The areas of the palace which are closed for reasons of safety and protection are accessible only to scholars and researchers having obtained special permission from the Directorate of the Archaeological Services in Herakleion. The closed areas around the palace can only be seen by visitors accompanied by the responsible custodian and guide.

The route which is suggested here for visiting the palace and the surrounding houses takes approximately two hours. To visit the outlying areas, a further hour and the use of a car are necessary.

INTRODUCTION

THE NATURAL ENVIRONMENT
HISTORY OF THE EXCAVATIONS
MYTHS AND LEGENDS

THE NATURAL ENVIRONMENT

The low hill, on which the Neolithic settlement of Knossos developed and where the great palace was later built, was called "Tjelebis Kefala" from the name of the Turkish landowner who sold the area to Sir Arthur Evans. During Minoan times, the hill was the nucleus of the town which also extended over the surrounding hills. In post-Minoan times, the hill with the ruins of the palace was part of the city-state of Knossos, probably remaining unbuilt, perhaps as a place of worship dedicated to the Mother Goddess.

The "Kefala" of Knossos is situated in the hilly inland area south of the valleys of Herakleion and Karteros. Through it runs the Kairatos river and its tributary, the Therron, 15 kilometres long, which rises in Archanes and flows into the sea at Poros, east of Herakleion. The port of Knossos was situated at the mouth of the Kairatos - the area known today as Katsambas and Poros.

East of the hill where the palace was built, rises mount Ai-Lias, as it is known locally (the mountain of the Prophet Elijah), a long and narrow calcareous hill, 300 metres high, covered with olive groves on its western side. A strong ancient wall stands on the side facing the palace.The marly limestone rocks of the hill were used as building material for the palace. High up on the hill opposite the palace stands the church of Aghia Paraskevi, which was built on the site of a Byzantine church with wall paintings, mentioned by the 15th century traveller, Ch. Buondelmonti.

To the north of the Head is the low hill of Djafer Papoura, and the hill of the Venizeleion University of Crete, and to the south are situated the Upper and Lower Gypsades, composed in the higher parts of crystalline gypsum rocks which were used in the building of the palace. To the west is the Acropolis (Monastiriako Kefali). The lower slopes of these hills are of soft yellowish-white limestone, exceptionally well-suited to the cultivation of olive trees and vines.

In the past few decades, with the use of machinery in farming, the natural environment of Knossos has undergone several changes. The waters of the Kaira-

tos, of course, no longer flow throughout the year, as in antiquity. Cultivated areas were fewer then, and the higher parts of the hills were covered with forests of cypress and oak. The climate of Knossos is characteristically Mediterranean. The average rainfall in Herakleion, occurring mainly during the period between October and March, is 477 mm. The mean annual temperature ranges from 12° Celsius in January to 26° Celsius in July.

HISTORY OF THE EXCAVATIONS

The first archaeological research, although amateur, as is natural, was conducted in 1878 by Minos Kalokairinos, a merchant from Herakleion, who uncovered a portion of the western storerooms of the Palace. He donated one each of the "pithoi" (large storage jars) which he discovered to the London, Paris, Rome and Athens museums. Also one to the Crown Prince of Greece, Constantine, and three to the collection of the Herakleion Educational Asociation. The remainder of the finds he kept in his own home in Herakleion, where they were destroyed during the 1898 uprising. The finds had been published by the Frenchman Haussoulier and the German, Fabricius. The discoveries of Minos Kalokairinos stimulated the interest of many prospective diggers, who attempted to buy the area of the palace from its Turkish owners. These were the American Consul W.J. Stillman, Heinrich Schliemann, the excavator of Troy and of Mycenae, who came to Crete together with his collaborator W. Doerpfeld in 1886, and the French archaeologist M. Joubin. All of them were unsuccessful in their negotiations with the owners.

The British archaeologist **A.J. Evans** was more successful. He bought the site and began digging in 1900, after the liberation of Crete from the Turks. He obtained permission to dig from the Cretan state and used his own funds for the excavation work. Within three years (1900-1902), the

CHRONOLOGICAL TABLE OF THE HISTORY OF CRETE

NEOLITHIC AGE (5700 -2800 BC)
BRONZE AGE (2800 - 1100 BC)
a. Prepalatial period (2800 - 1900 BC) **b.** Old Palace period (1900 - 1700 BC)
c. New Palace period (1700 - 1400 BC) **d.** Postpalatial period (1400 - 1100 BC)

IRON AGE (1100 - 67 BC)
a. Sub-Minoan and Early Geometric period (1100 - 900 BC)
b. Geometric period (900 - 750 BC)
c. Early Archaic period (750 - 650 BC)
d. Late Archaic period (650 - 500 BC)
e. Classical period (500 - 323 BC)
f. Hellenistic period (323 - 67 BC)

GRECO-ROMAN PERIOD (67 BC - 323 AD)

FIRST BYZANTINE PERIOD (323 - 824 BC)

THE PERIOD OF ARAB RULE - THE BYZANTINE PERIOD - THE PERIOD OF VENETIAN RULE (826 - 1669 AD)

THE PERIOD OF TURKISH OCCUPATION (1669 - 1898 AD)

Note: A second chronologial system proposed by A. Evans is also used for the Bronze Age, mainly for the dating of pottery. According to this system, there are three main periods which are each subdivided into three phases (Early Minoan I-III, Middle Minoan I-III, Late Minoan I-III etc.)

13

Sir Arthur Evans, who excavated Knossos

greater part of the palace had come to light. In the following years, complementary excavations inside the palace were carried out, and the houses around the palace were uncovered, as well as the extensive burial grounds of Minoan Knossos. After a temporary halt between 1912-1922, the work was resumed until 1931, when the "southern royal tomb" was excavated. Apart from the excavation works, Sir Arthur Evans undertook the ambitious and important task of partially reconstructing and restoring the palace. A task, unique in so far as a large prehistoric monument is concerned, and one which he carried out with great daring, knowledge and imagination. Without Arthur Evans' restoration, our knowledge of the Minoan civilization would be very scant. Although he was much criticized - perhaps not entirely unjustly - for excesses, yet his restoration remained valuable and useful for many decades. We must not forget, of course, that it was undertaken eighty years ago, and

that today other views on the subject of restoration of monuments prevail.

Sir Arthur Evans was assisted by several eminent archaeologists: **D. Mackenzie, D. Hogarth, Alan Wace, J. Forsdyke** and later **John Pendlebury, H. Payne** and **R. Hutchinson.** Among his close collaborators were also the architects **Th. Fyfe, Chr. Doll, F. Newton** and **Piet de Jong** as well as **Gillieron** father and son, the painters. It is to the latter that we owe the marvellous reconstructions of the palace and of the palace frescoes.

Between 1921 and 1935, Sir Arthur Evans published the finds from his excavations in his monumental, six-volume work, THE PALACE OF MINOS AT KNOSSOS, a work which constitutes the "Bible" of Minoan archaeology. He also published many books and essays on Minoan Crete. Few scholars have been so honoured during their lifetime as was Sir Arthur Evans, who died, at a ripe old age, in 1941.

After the Second World War, other British archaeologists continued to excavate on the palace site and in the surrounding areas. They were led by **S. Hood,** the most authoritative living scholar on Minoan civilization. Hood conducted additional excavations in and around the palace, so as to solve many questions of archaeological research at Knossos. Apart from his three general books on Minoan civilization (see Bi-

bliography), he drew accurate plans of the palace ruins and was in charge of the archaeological topographical charting of the Knossos area. Alongside S. Hood and after him, several eminent archaeologists carried out research at Knossos: **J. Evans** systematically studied the neolithic strata of the western and central courts of the palace. **N. Coldstream** excavated the sanctuary of Demeter at Gypsades and **M. Gough** the Villa Dionysus. **M. Popham** and **H. Sackett** uncovered the Unexplored Mansion by the

Little Palace. **Peter Warren** dug along the "Royal Way" and south of the Villa Ariadne. This research was recently resumed by **C. Macdonal**d, west of the palace.

The Knossos excavations, as is the case with all archaeological sites, also have their unseen protagonists. Here we shall mention in order of seniority the unforgettable skilled workmen and overseers: Manolis Akoumianakis, Manolis Markogiannakis, Spyros A. Vassilakis, Antonis Zidianakis and the restorer Petros Petrakis. Let me be allowed to dedicate this book to their memory.

Sir Arthur Evans initially used as his "headquarters" the house of a Turkish bey to the southeast of the palace. Later he built the Villa Ariadne which he himself and the British School of Archaeology used until 1952, when it was ceded to the Greek state. Since then, the British School is housed in the buildings of the "Taverna" of the Villa Ariadne. The finds from both the older and the more recent excavations are kept in the Stratigraphic Museum, which was built in 1964, south of the Villa Ariadne.

During the first decades after the Second World War, **Nikolaos Platon** and **Stylianos Alexiou** undertook much consolidation and restoration work as well as additional research. In 1976, by a Presidential Decree, the erection of buildings in the area was only allowed within the limits of the existing settlements and a very broad space was defined in which construction was prohibited, so as to protect the unique archaeological site of Knossos.

During the past ten years, archaeologists of the Herakleion Ephorate of Antiquities have been carrying out rescue excavations in plots of land where construction is going on at Knossos, as well as in the northern cemetery (area of the University of Crete) where a number of tombs dating from the period between 1100 BC to AD 400 are being uncovered.

In the 1980s the consolidation and conservation of the palace structures began to be planned. These structures had started to show signs of considerable wear, mainly due to the great number of people visiting the site. It is expected that the restoration work will begin soon.

MYTHS AND LEGENDS ASSOCIATED WITH KNOSSOS

The plot and action of many ancient Greek myths are set on Crete, and revolve around the king of Knossos, **Minos**, son of **Zeu**s and of **Europa**, the Phoenician nymph. Minos and his brothers **Rhadamanthy**s and **Sarpedon**, were born on Crete, and according to one story, in the region of Gortyn. After being abandoned by Zeus,

Theseus and the Minotaur, depicted on a red-figure vase

Europa and Zeus-the Bull, depicted on a red-figure vase

17

Theseus and Ariadne, depicted on a vase from Arkades

Europa married **Asterius**, the king of Crete, who adopted her sons. Asterius was succeeded on the throne by Minos.

Minos married **Pasiphaë**, daughter of Helios, the sun-god, and of the nymph Crete, and of this marriage were born four sons and four daughters, Catreus, Xenodike, Ariadne, Androgeus, Glaucus, Deucalion, Phaedra and Acalle (or Acaccalis).

A number of dramatic events took place in the palace of Knossos. Minos dedicated an altar to Poseidon, and after he had made all the preparations for the sacrifice, he asked the god to cause a bull to spring from the sea. Minos was so stunned by the beauty of the white bull which emerged

from the sea, that he broke his promise and sacrificed another bull in its place. To punish him, Poseidon instilled a passionate love for the bull in the heart of Pasiphaë. She confided her love to **Daedalus**, the renowned Athenian craftsman, who created for her a carved wooden image of a cow covered in real hide. The queen hid inside it and thus mated with the divine bull. From their union was born the **Minotaur**, a man with the head of a bull, who was also given the name of Asterius. He was imprisoned by Minos in the maze-like building, the Labyrinth, created by Daedalus.

One of the sons of Minos, Androgeus, was killed in Athens, after having won in the Athenian games. His murder was the cause of Minos' imposing on the Athenians the obligation to send seven youths and seven maidens every ninth year, to be devoured by the Minotaur. This is where the Athenian hero, **Theseus** - who, according to one tradition, was a son of Poseidon - comes into the myth. Theseus offered himself as one of the victims to be sent to Crete. There, **Ariadne** fell in love with him and, together with Daedalus, helped him enter the Labyrinth and kill the Minotaur, thus putting an end to the tribute of blood. Theseus left Crete together with his companions and with Ariadne whom, in compliance with the will of the gods, he abandoned on the island of Naxos to Dionysus. From the union of Dionysus and Ariadne were born Staphylos, Thoas and Oenopion.

The myth of prince **Glaucus** is also a colourful and interesting one. Glaucus was being initiated into the art of divination by **Polyeidos**, the seer from Argos. As the young prince was playing in the palace one day, he drowned in a jar used for storing honey. King Minos ordered Polyeidos to bring him back to life and locked them both up in a tomb. Polyeidos managed to restore Glaucus to life by using a herb brought to him by a serpent. After this, the seer taught Glaucus his art but, when he was leaving to return to his country, Argos, and was about to embark, he asked

The Minotaur on a silver coin

Glaucus to spit into his mouth, whereupon Glaucus lost all his divinatory powers.

The mythological cycle closes with the dramatic escape of **Daedalus** and his son **Icarus** from Crete, with wings made by Daedalus himself. Icarus fell into the sea, which took his name - the Icarian Sea - and was drowned. Daedalus sought refuge in Sicily, where he was pursued by king Minos. With the help of a Sicilian princess, however, and of king Cocalus, he managed to escape and, using a cunning trick, to murder Minos. The king was buried with great pomp by his followers in Sicily, where the town of Minoa was founded in his honour. After his death, both he and his brother Rhadamanthys were deified and became divine judges of souls in Hades, together with Aeacus, grandfather of Achilles. According to another version of the myth, Daedalus left Crete with Icarus not with the help of artificial wings but on a boat. As they were sailing east of the Cyclades, Icarus tripped, fell into the sea and was drowned. His father buried him on the nearest island, which took the name of Icaria. After this, he continued sailing to the west, to Sicily.

Another famous king of Crete was **Idomeneus**, grandson of Minos, and son of Deucalion. Idomeneus took part in the Trojan War, where he distinguished himself and was the third strongest and bravest of the Greek leaders. Idomeneus personifies the dynamism of Crete during the Mycenean period. As is the case with all myths, those of Knossos do not themselves constitute history, but they do conceal, in their core, certain historical facts. Knowledge of these myths help in the study and understanding of many questions regarding the Minoan civilization. Thus, Ariadne, the young heroine from Knossos who dies on the island of Dia, now known as Naxos, is the personification of the young goddess of fruitful growth who dies and is reborn each year, following the cycle of nature. The mythical labyrinth is the palace of Knossos itself, with its unique complexity. In the personality of Daedalus we find condensed the essence of the technological development and progress of the Minoans. The story about the Athenian youths and maidens who were offered in tribute to the Minotaur, awakens echoes of the famous "taurokathapsia" (bull-leaping)*, of which the Minoans were very fond, but also indicates the influence exercised by Knossos over the entire southern part of Greece all the way to Athens. Europa, to whom our continent owes its name, was the mother of the divine Minos, who in turn gave the first European civilization its name. Minos was perhaps the title of the kings of Knossos, as the title of "Pharaoh" was that of Egyptian kings. Alternatively, there may have been one or more kings of this name. What is more important is that in the figure of Minos, the ancient Greeks saw a powerful ruler, an inspired law-giver, an equitable judge, the sovereign of the largest portion of the Greek world, that is of southern, central and eastern Greece and the Aegean, during the period when the Minoan civilization was at the acme of its development.

*athletic contests, probably of a religious nature, in which both men and women took part.

HISTORICAL
DEVELOPMENT

HISTORICAL DEVELOPMENT

Knossos, on Crete, was one of the most ancient cities of the Aegean and of Europe. The vast site over which the ruins lie, at a distance of approximately 5 kilometres from Herakleion, the modern capital of Crete, is visited every day by thousands of people from all over the world. They come to see and to admire the remains of this brilliant and refined ancient Greek civilization. There has been a constant human presence on this site for about eight thousand years, from 6000 BC to our day. This long course of mankind in this favoured corner of the earth we shall now follow in a brief narration.

THE NEOLITHIC AGE
(circa 5700 - 2800 BC)

The low hill of Knossos was first inhabited shortly after 6000 BC. Within three thousand years it had become the largest Neolithic settlement on Crete and in the Aegean.

The Neolithic strata have been fully and systematically explored and we thus have a good deal of information on the life of these ancient ancestors of the Greeks. In a short period of time, taking advantage of the stability which prevailed in the area after the last Ice Age, the inhabitants of Neolithic Knossos developed a mixed economy based on agriculture and cattle-raising. They were also adept in handicrafts. The clay pottery they produced, after their initial trials, was created with astonishing artistry. The fabrication of stone tools had reached a high technological level. Implements were made not only of wood but also of animal bones and horns. Other interesting finds are the wooden and clay figurines, representing male and female forms. The houses built by the inhabitants of Knossos, which were composed of small rooms around a larger, central room, were

Steatite rhyton in the shape of a bull's head

Plan of Neolithic buildings

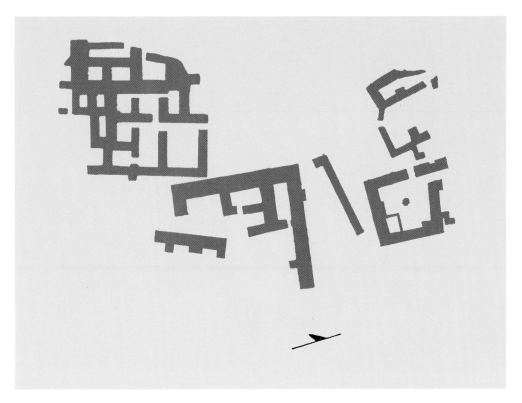

Neolithic vase with incised decoration

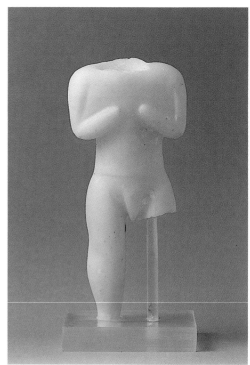

Neolithic marble figurine

Neolithic axes

The circular repositories in the west court

made of mud bricks, which had been dried in the sun, set on stone foundations. The area of the Neolithic settlement, around 3000 BC, was approximately the same as that of the later palace. The Neolithic strata of Knossos have only partially survived. Below the central court of the palace, the strata which have come to light belong to the Mesolithic period, owing either to the extensive use or to the levelling of the ruins of the Neolithic settlement when the first palace came to be built.

The Neolithic period at Knossos and more generally on Crete coincides with a relatively advanced stage of civilization, when metals were unknown. The knowledge and use of metals, and primarily of bronze, marks the beginning of the next stage of civilization.

THE BRONZE AGE (circa 2800 - 1100 BC)
This period, which lasted for approximately 2000 years, was the first great and brilliant period of Cretan civilization, and indeed, of the entire Greek world. In Crete, during these centuries, was born, grew, developed and reached its culmination the first Greek cultural miracle of the Aegean world, the Minoan civilization.

The development of this civilization can be divided into four chronological periods, distinguished on the basis of the key events of its historical course, such as the foundation, the destruction, the recon-

25

Vase in the floral style

The Prepalatial period

The visitors to Knossos do not see the ruins of the Prepalatial period, since these were levelled in order to erect the great palace. However, we know from the excavations carried out, that a large prepalatial settlement existed here. Houses belonging to this settlement were uncovered to the north and south of the Royal Way. Sir Arthur Evans and S. Hood found sections of a large building of the late prepalatial years in the western court and below the Western Magazines of the palace.

Excavation of the prepalatial settlement is difficult because of the existence of buildings of later periods over them.

The period of the old palace

The foundation of the palace at Knossos, as is the case with that of the other Cretan centres, was an event of the highest historic, political, economic and social importance, and the natural development and consequence of the economic and cultural flowering which took place in the previous period.

The palaces were the centre of all the life and activities of the city-state. In them were stored and kept, under the protection of the deity, the produce of the land and the animals, in which the palace traded. Here, too, in separate areas, were work-

struction and the final devastation of the palace.

The periods of the Minoan civilization, according to the chronological system of Professor N. Platon, are the following (in brackets, the corresponding subdivisions as devised by Sir Arthur Evans):

PREPALATIAL PERIOD 2800-1900 BC (Early Minoan I, II, and II and Middle Minoan IA)

PROTOPALATIAL PERIOD 1900-1700 BC (Middle Minoan IB, Middle Minoan II)

NEOPALATIAL PERIOD 1700-1400 BC (Middle Minoan III, Late Minoan I and II)

POSTPALATIAL PERIOD 1400-1100 BC (Late Minoan III)

(See Indexes)

shops where were created the wonderful pottery, stonework, small objects of art and jewellery we see today. The palace was not only the residence of the members of the royal family, but also that of a numerous administrative and religious hierarchy. Very little has survived of the old palace of Knossos, owing to the fact that on its site was built the new palace.

Its dimensions and plan, with its two large courts, were perhaps the same as those of the later palace. Today, it is thought that it was a single building complex. Sir Arthur Evans, on the other hand, had put forward the theory of the *insulae*, that is of independent large buildings which were gradually linked. Generally speaking, and with a good degree of certainty, we now believe that the storerooms were also situated in the western wing, while in the northeastern part were situated the workshops and the royal magazines, where the giant pithoi (storage jars) were found. The shrines were also situated in the western wing, as were the shrines of the later palace. Around the palace were built retaining walls, and there was a courtyard on the western side. In the western court there were built circular pits, known as "kouloures", which served as refuse or sewage dumps. These pits were covered in the period of the new palace.

Very little is known about the city of the old palace period, although it is certain that it was already large and extensive. The royal way and the courts were perhaps paved during this period. The big viaduct to the south of the palace dates from this period. The cemeteries of the city were situated on the flanks of the Ai-Lias hill. They consisted of cave-tombs with a great many pithos burials.

Despite the lack of very much evidence on the Knossos of this period, it was already the great capital of Crete, with links with Archanes, Lykastos and Phaestos, but also with centres of the Aegean, Egypt and the East.

Kamares ware vase

The period of the new palace

The old palace was completely destroyed around 1700 BC, after it had twice already suffered more limited damage. The problem of how and why this destruction occurred is a complex one. Usually this kind of destruction is attributed to natural phenomena, such as earthquakes and fires. The new palace was built according to a new set of plans, since the hilltop was levelled again and the palace erected on the fill. A deep cutting was also made on the eastern side of the hill, and on the lower level, eight metres down, which was thus formed, were built the royal apartments of the eastern wing. The new palace covered a total area of 22,000 m² (or about 5,5 acres). This palace also was destroyed three times. The greater part of the ruins which are visible today, belong to the second phase of the new palace (1600 - 1500 BC). During the next phases several changes were made to parts of the palace, but these did not significantly alter its general structure. They will be referred to later in special chapters of this guide. Here, only the general picture presented by the palace around 1500 BC will be given, as well as its basic and characteristic elements.

One could enter the palace of Knossos through any one of five entrances: the northern one, the southern one, the northwestern one, the southwestern one and the eastern one. The first four were the more formal entrances, with propyla and wide portals. To the west of the palace extended the paved west court, traversed by processional ways. In this area two altars had been built. In the southwestern corner of the court was the western entrance. It had a pillared propylon and led, from the south, along a wide processional corridor in the shape of the Greek letter Π, to the central court, at the spot where the reproduction of the fresco of the "priest prince" can be seen today.

There was another monumental entrance to the south (great propylaea). This was where the stepped portico, which led from the guest house to the south across the

viaduct, ended up. From the great propylaea a grand staircase led to the first floor of the west wing (piano nobile). This wing had large ceremonial rooms on the top floor. On the ground floor were situated the magazines, the shrines, the treasuries and the throne room.

In the northern section were the magazines, a lustral area which has been restored today, and the customs house. On either side of an inclined corridor leading from the customs house to the central court there were impressive balconies, one of which, adorned with a bull in relief, has been restored.

Outside the northwestern corner of the palace was situated the theatre built of stone, where ended the royal road which passed through the city from the northwest.

The "royal apartments" were situated in the eastern wing. To the north of these, were the workshops and to the south a shrine. Some of the houses in the southeastern corner, outside the palace, have been excavated.

The Minoan city and its cemeteries

During the Neopalatial period, Knossos was at the height of its splendour. Around the palace, mainly to the west and north, but also in the lower parts of the hills of the Acropolis and Gypsades, lay the city with the large houses for the priests, the officials and the middle class. All of these were grand and impressive in construction, and adorned with beautiful frescoes.

According to Sir Arthur Evans, the town extended over an area of 125,000 m². Its population he estimated at 80 - 100,000 inhabitants (though these numbers seem rather exaggerated). Other figures, proposed by S. Hood, according to whom the area of Minoan Knossos was 75,000 m² and its population 15 - 20,000, seem a more realistic estimate.

The seaport of Knossos was also a portion of the great city. It was situated where the eastern quarters of Herakleion, Poros - Ka-

tsamba are today. The port was situated at the site of Trypiti (today the area has been much altered in aspect, owing to the construction of the extension of the new port and the coastal avenue). On the level land where the Kairatos flows out into the sea, stood the houses of the rich merchants and seamen of Knossos. Their tombs, where many funeral gifts were found, were cut into the hillsides. During the past decades, finds of significant importance have been uncovered in houses and tombs.

The **cemeteries** of Knossos extend in every direction on the hillsides, as far as the modern suburb of Aghios Ioannis, two and a half kilometres north of the palace. Most of the tombs are rock-cut chamber tombs, but there were also some more monumental built tombs, such as the southern royal grave-sanctuary at Gypsades, the royal tomb at Isopata (this was destroyed during the German occupation), the tholos tombs at Kefala and Gypsades.

Much of the road network of the ancient city is not known to us. The royal way, which follows a northwesterly direction, has been uncovered, as well as a portion of its extension in the area west of the Stratigraphical Museum. Unlike what has been the case at other Minoan sites, at Knossos we are unable to say what the town plan was like, since no suburb of the city has been brought to light in its entirety.

The irrigation and drainage system at Knossos is most interesting. The aqueduct supplied water through tubular conduits from a great distance (from the Kounavoi and Archanes regions) and branched out inside the city and the palace, where parts of the drainage system have been found. There were two built drainage channels, one to collect the sewage and the other the rain water, which passed through the palace and led off the water.

This was the period when the palace and the city were at the height of their glory. The inhabitants of Knossos, like all the Minoans, lived happily on their blessed land. They worshipped the Mother Goddess in her shrines, in homes and outdoors. Their carts and pack animals car-

The throne room

ried produce to the palace and the port. Their ships sailed back and forth across the seas, over which Crete dominated, and carried her products to every part of the known world. In exchange, they brought back to the island many raw materials.

The "Mycenean" palace

This happy life in the palace and in the city was rudely shattered by a natural phenomenon, known from the past. Around 1450 BC, according to the most prevalent theory, all the palatial cities of Crete were destroyed by an earthquake and fire. The palace managed to withstand the shock and went on living, after some repairs and alterations, for another 50-70

Pithoi of the period of the reoccupation from the south propylaea

years, until 1400/1380 BC.

Our knowledge concerning this last phase in the life of the palace of Knossos (Late Minoan II according to Arthur Evans' classification), is mainly based on archaeological evidence (pottery and architecture), but also on the tablets inscribed in Linear B script which were found in the palace. The main conclusion is that a Mycenean *anax* (king) had installed himself in the palace of Knossos, which was, during this period, the only palatial centre in Crete. We do not know under what circumstances this dynastic

33

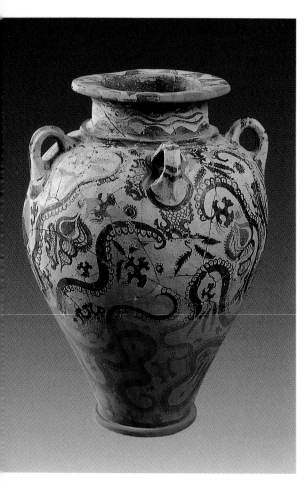

Vase in the "Marine" style

general spirit is militaristic, in obvious contrast to that of the peace-loving Minoans. Burials of warriors take place at Knossos (in the Venizeleion area of today). The *anax* of Knossos is the overlord of the entire island. From clay tablets we know the names of the cities which are under the control of Knossos: Amnissos and Tylissos, Phaestos and Inatos, Lyktos, Lato, Siteia and Itanos, Sybrita, Kydonia, Aptera. They raise sheep and send the wool to the palace. Commerce is once again in the hands of the king, as in previous years. Relations with Egypt and with the rest of the known world are close.

Everyday life remained purely Minoan, basically. The Myceneans were satisfied with retaining suzerainty over the island. Religion, too, remained Minoan, although new divinities were introduced.

The post palatial period

Around 1400/1380 BC a new disaster befell Knossos. Some scholars date it to the end of the 14th or the beginning of the 13th century (just before or just after 1300 BC). Its causes are not entirely known. The fire which devastated the palace has been attributed to an accidental cause or to a revolt of the subjugated Minoans of Knossos against the Myceneans, who came from mainland Greece. The final obliteration of Mycenean Knossos, which until then had still been powerful, was thus brought about. Whatever the cause may have been, the majority of scholars agree that the palace of Knossos ceased to exist - at least in the form in which we know it - after these disastrous events. In the years which followed, the ruins of the palace were for a time "reoccupied" by private individuals, who brought about some alterations to various parts of the structure. The southern propylaea were used as storerooms and a pottery work-shop was installed in the queen's megaron. In the Homeric epics, which are usually con-sidered to be a source of information on the later phase of the Minoan and Mycenean periods, the personage of Idomeneus is mentioned as being king of Knossos and of Crete. The site of

change took place. It has been attributed to military conquest, to peaceful inter-marriage or to a coup by a Mycenean general of the Minoan navy. It is a fact, in any case, that the Myceneans took advant-age of the shock which followed the dis-aster to establish themselves at Knossos.

Various alterations were then made to the palace: the throne room was incorporated into the old structure and adorned with frescoes showing a Mycenean influence. In pottery, the Mycenean influence is even more apparent (Palace style). The Linear B script of the tablets found in the palace has been deciphered. It is the earliest known form of the Greek language. The

Idomeneus' palace remains an unsolved problem. If we accept that this was Mycenean Knossos, we must also accept that the palace was standing here until the second half of the 13th century BC.

The splendid Minoan palace, after six centuries of grandeur, ended up as a desolate ruin. Only the ghosts of its old glory remained, to haunt the ruined staircases and passages, the megara and shrines, to mourn the brilliant past. It was perhaps the extent and impressive intricacy of the ruins which gave birth to the myth of the Labyrinth.

THE "CITY-STATE" OF KNOSSOS

The Early Iron Age

Bronze Age Knossos was succeeded, on the same site, by the city-state of Knossos, which lasted for a period of approximately 1000 years. The palace area was considered sacred and the ruins were not inhabited. According to the historian, Diodorus, it was the sacred wood of Rhea, and the site of a small temple dedicated to the goddess. Now the nucleus of the city was to be found to the north and west of the position of the old palace, near which there were three temples or sanctuaries: that of Demeter at Gypsades, that of Rhea on the palace site itself, and that of Zeus and Hera on the so-called acropolis. What remains unknown is the location of the seat of the local king or lord and that of the city's agora. Better known are the extensive cemeteries in what is today the area of the Venizeleion and the University, and still further to the north. It is estimated that the city covered an area of 500,000 - 600,000 m^2 and had a corresponding number of inhabitants. It may have been organized on the basis of separate large villages which were dependent on a central town, situated to the west and north of the site of the palace. The cultural and artistic influence of Knossos extended throughout the entire island, in which it held the position of metropolis. Knossos' relations with the other important centres in Greece and the East were also very close.

The Classical and Hellenistic periods

Knossos was one of the most important cities in Crete, a friend and ally alternately of the other important cities of Gortyn, Lyktos, Kydonia. There was perhaps a period during which the city fell into decline, probably after some calamity. From these four centuries only a few ruins are known to us, the sanctuaries, the temples, the *heroa*, the cemeteries. In the southwestern part of the area of the "Villa Ariadne", and to the west of the settlement of today at the foot of the acropolis, were situated potters' workshops. Of the sanctuaries which existed during the previous period, those still in use were the temple of Demeter on the modern site of

Vase of the Geometric period

35

Metope of a temple with a scene from the myth of the Erymanthian boar

THE GRECO-ROMAN PERIOD

During the 2nd and the beginning of the 1st century BC, Knossos was the proud and powerful Cretan city which stood up to the Roman conquerors. Her resistance cost her her undisputed, until then, pre-eminent position in Crete. A position which after the Roman conquest of 67 BC was held by Gortyn. The status of Knossos was now that of a Roman "colony". Its area is estimated at approximately 500,000 - 600,000 m². It was, however, a flourishing city with splendid public buildings and private houses. Their ruins are still to be seen today at the site now known as Hellenika, between the area of the Venizeleion and

Gypsades, the temple of Rhea on the palace site, the *heroon* of Glaucus in today's settlement of Bougada Metochi, two temples on the "acropolis" which have been identified with the temple of Zeus and Hera, and the temple of the Delphic Apollo as well as one more temple in the region known today as Tekés. The structural remains of sanctuaries and temples are scant, but inscriptions and architectural elements have been discovered (metopes, cornices etc.).

that of the "Villa Ariadne". The mosaics of the "Villa Dionysus" are among the best of the Roman Imperial period. Sections of a large aqueduct of Roman times have been uncovered at Spelia, south of Knossos. Many graves of a variety of types dating to this period have been excavated. They range from simple, tile-covered graves to rock-cut chamber tombs, as well as underground or ground-level mausoleums. One of these mausoleums is that known as "Caiaphas' grave", which was studied by S. Xanthoudides but has not survived to our day. A mausoleum recently excavated by the present writer has been preserved at the northern entrance of the University.

THE FIRST BYZANTINE PERIOD

In the early centuries of Christianity, Knossos was an important centre and the see of a bishop. Archaeological research has discovered three churches, of the basilica type: one in the area of the Venizeleion Hospital with mosaics, a second one in the Makrys Toichos settlement, where the church of Aghia Sophia stands today, and a third one, a cemetery church, on the University grounds. At some point in time before the 9th century AD, the see of the bishop of Knossos was transferred to Raukos, to the site where the village of Aghios Myronas

Maleviziou now stands. The administrative centre also was transferred to the port of Knossos, which is today Herakleion. The city gradually shrunk into a small settlement, on the site of the place we now know as Makrys Toichos (Long Wall).

THE PERIOD OF ARAB DOMINATION - THE BYZANTINE PERIOD - THE PERIOD OF VENETIAN RULE

During the period of Arab domination, only a few huts stood on the site of the settlement of Makrys Toichos. In the middle Byzantine period and during the period of Venetian rule, there was a settlement around the church on the site of the basilica of Aghia Sophia. This is perhaps the church mentioned by Buondelmonti. However, according to another opinion, the traveller was referring to the

The labyrinth
on a silver coin

The head of Zeus-Minos
on a silver coin

CA N

Engraving of Candia (Herakleion)
Benaki Museum, Athens

Byzantine church of Aghia Paraskevi at
Ai-Lias. He also mentions the grave of
Caiaphas who, according to a local legend,
was buried in Knossos. During the Venetian period, the settlement of Makrys
Toichos was recorded as having 150 inhabitants.

THE PERIOD OF OTTOMAN
OCCUPATION

The small village of Makrys Toichos was
renamed by the Turks Bougada Metochi,
from the name of the Bougada river
(Tchamashir Déré) - the ancient Kairatos.
The name "Bougada", which means the
"wash", is owed to the fact that the Turks
of the Fortezza military camp used to do
their washing here, during the siege of the

town of Candia (Herakleion).

At the end of the 19th century (1881), a
number of small settlements or "metochia" had been registered in the area of
ancient Knossos: Hellenika to the north,
Makrys Toichos to the northeast and
Metochia (monastery dependencies) to the
west and south of the palace hill. The
Makrys Toichos settlement is the oldest in
the area, and its church (Aghia Sophia) is
built on the site of the early Christian
basilica. It owes its name to a long wall at
Hellenika and Topana, which may have
been part of a large building of Roman
times. Makrys Toichos and the metochia
had a population of 154 inhabitants (65 of
whom were Christians and 89 Muslims),
and came under the jurisdiction of the
Municipality of Archanes. After 1900, the
new settlement of Knossos, west of the

palace, reverted to its old name of Bougada Metochi. The metochi south of the palace, on the eastern flank of Gypsades, was named Vlychia, from the brackish spring of the same name (vlychó = brackish) which welled from the site of the Minoan guest house but which ran dry a few years ago.

KNOSSOS IN THE 20TH CENTURY

The metochia of the region of Knossos later came under the jurisdiction of the Municipality of Herakleion, and its ancient name began once more to be used, although the old names were not forgotten. In the early part of our century, Evans carried out his extensive excavations which changed the fate of the site and of the entire island.

Evans' first "headquarters" were in a "konak", a large house, to the southeast of the palace hill. Later, the Villa Ariadne - known to the locals as the "Villa" was built to serve as the central office of the archaeological mission of Knossos. In 1952 the villa was ceded to the Greek State.

In May 1941, during the Battle of Crete, the Greek king, George, and the Tsouderos government used the Villa Ariadne as their base for a short time. One of the confrontations between the German forces and the people of Crete defending their homeland during the Battle of Crete, took place in the area of Knossos.

During the German Occupation, the High Command of the German forces in Crete made the Villa Ariadne their headquarters. Today, the two sections of the settlement of Knossos have a steady population of about 400 inhabitants, involved in farming and tourism.

GUIDE

THE PALACE
THE HOUSES AROUND THE PALACE

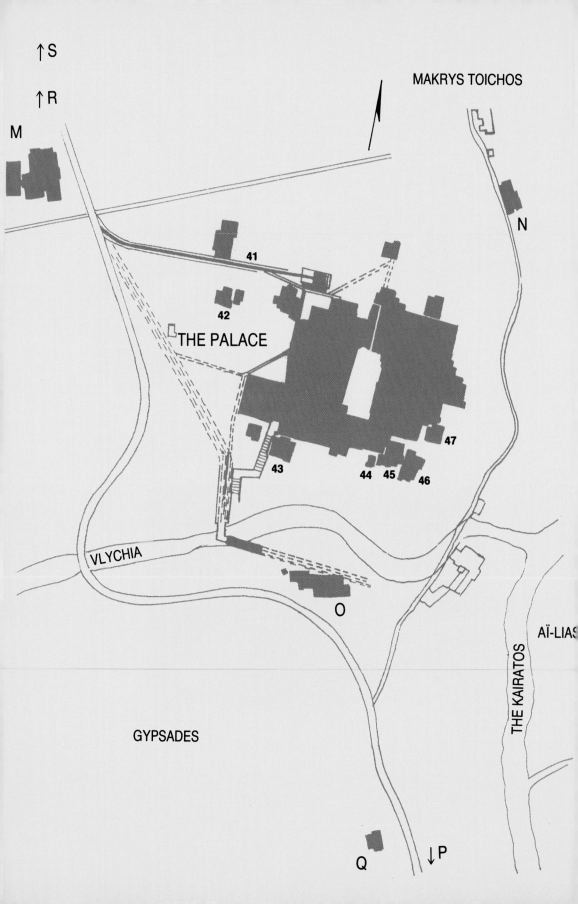

↑S

↑R

M

MAKRYS TOICHOS

N

41

42

THE PALACE

47

43

44 45 46

VLYCHIA

O

AÏ-LIAS

THE KAIRATOS

GYPSADES

Q   ↓P

VISITOR'S GUIDE

KNOSSOS

Knossos is one of the major archaeological sites in Greece in terms of its importance and interest to the visitor. This is because the mighty city of Minos and Ariadne, of Pasiphaë, the Minotaur and Idomeneus, was one of the first cities on European soil, a centre which radiated the light of one of the most brilliant civilizations of Greek and European prehistory - the Minoan civilization, named after the great god-king Minos. The ruins of this city, partially restored by Sir Arthur Evans, stand as irrefutable witnesses of its ancient splendour. The itinerary suggested by this guide is that most commonly used and is the most practical and logical. However, if the visitor wishes to do so, he can follow other possible routes. In the near future the visitors' route will undergo some alterations and some areas will be cordoned off. Generally speaking, the present route will be followed, however. After the tour of the palace and the houses around it in the main archaeological area, we recommend that visitors see another three large structures beyond this area: a tomb, and two monuments of Roman times, the Villa Dionysus and a mausoleum.

THE PALACE

To get to the main archaeological site, one follows the Herakleion-Viannos road. Outside the palace there is a parking lot. Beyond the entrance and the ticket booths, a refreshment bar and a stand where books and postcards are on sale, the palace tour begins.

WEST WING

The visitor today enters the palace area by a modern stepped construction, built on the site of the ancient western entrance and immediately finds himself in the great paved WEST COURT of the palace **(A)**, which is bounded on the western side by a retaining wall. At the further end, to the east, can be seen the partially restored western facade of the palace. Three **processional ways (3)** forming a triangle and raised slightly from the level of the ground, run across the court. In the southwestern corner stands the bust of Sir Arthur Evans, the archaeologist who excavated Knossos, placed there in his honour by the Municipality of Herakleion.

The West Court

The western façade of the palace

Topographical plan of the archaeological site

THE PALACE

A. WEST COURT
B. WEST MAGAZINES
C. THRONE ROOM COMPLEX
D. COMPLEX OF THE CENTRAL SHRINE
E. CENTRAL COURT
F. ROYAL APARTMENTS
G. SHRINE OF THE DOUBLE AXES
H. WORKSHOPS AREA
I. GREAT EAST HALL
J. NORTH ENTRANCE COMPLEX
K. NORTHWEST AREA
L. THEATRE

 1. The "kouloures"
 2. Altars
 3. Processional way
 4. West Entrance
 5. Processional way
 6. South Propylaea
 7. Grand Staircase
 8. Ceremonial halls
 9. Corridor of the Magazines
10. West staircase
11. Antechamber
12. Throne room
13. Lustral basin
14. Tripartite shrine
15. Temple repository
16. Pillar crypt
17. Site of Rhea's temple
18. South Entrance
19. Grand staircase
20-21. Hall of the Double Axes or King's Megaron
22. Queen's Megaron
23. Bench-altar
24. Lustral basin
25. Lapidary's workshop
26. Potter's workshop
27. Court of the Stone Spout
28. Magazine of the Giant Pithoi
29. East Entrance
30. Magazine of the Pithoi
31-32. Corridor of the Bays
33. Corridor of the Draughtboard
34. Magazines of the Old Palace
35. Northeast Magazines
36. Customs House
37. North Entrance
38. North lustral basin
39. Underground rooms
40. Theatre

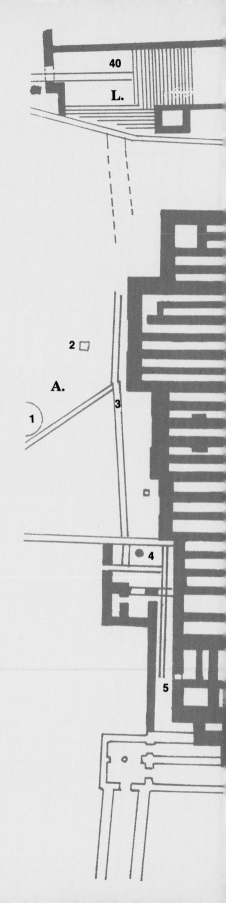

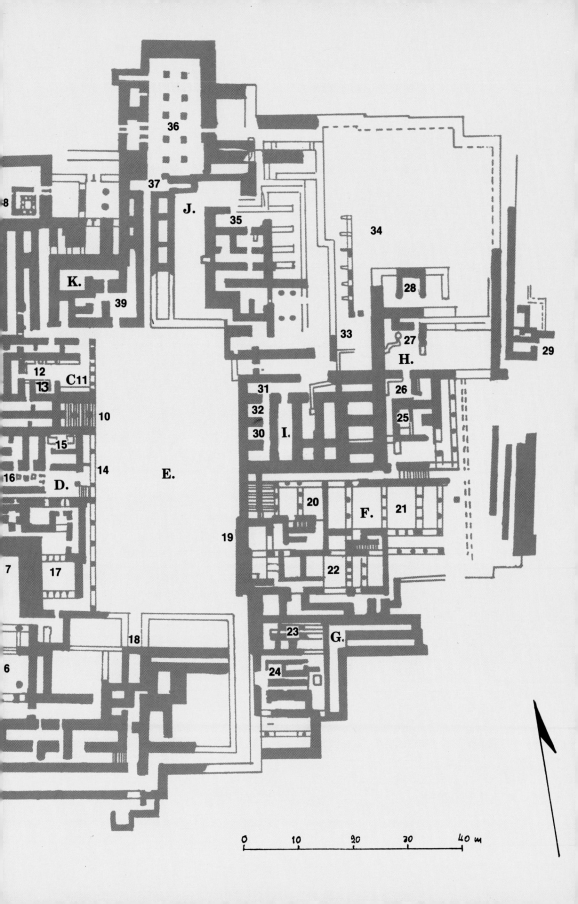

**The southwestern
corner of the palace**

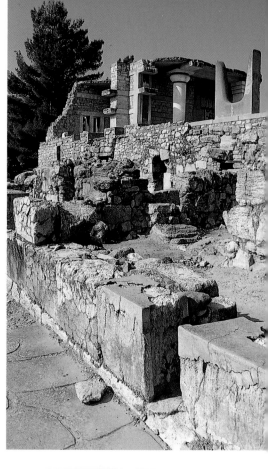

**The southern
facade of the palace**

**The great
south propylaea**

**The fresco of the
Prince with the Lilies**

**The fresco
of the rhyton-bearer**

The three large built pits we see, known as **"kouloures" (1)**, were intended to receive the refuse and the offerings from the ritual ceremonies which were held in the west court, as the two low built **altars (2)** there indicate. The west court had a formal and religious function and was linked by means of a processional way on its northern side to the "theatre". In the deeper strata under the court, the remains of the prepalatial and Neolithic settlements of the hill have been uncovered.

From the west court the visitor enters the palace, passing through the monumental **West Entrance (4)**, a columned portico (height of column = five metres), and the guard-room, and continues along the paved **processional way (5)**, whose walls were adorned with the famous frescoes of the Procession. The corridor has not been

**Reproduction of the stepped portico
(according to K. Iliakis)**

The south entrance

The western magazines

restored in its southern section and the visitor thus makes his way through a narrow passage to come to the wide South **Propylaea (6)**. Here ended the stepped portico which led from the guest house over the viaduct, and which constituted the initial south entrance. After its destruction around 1600 BC, a new smaller south entrance was built, which led, through an L- shaped corridor to the southwestern corner of the central court. The western section of the south propylaea has been restored, and this is where a reproduction of part of the fresco of the Procession has been placed. The south propylaea had two columns in the front and back of the wide gate, which shut from the south. The pithoi which are in the propylaea belong to the period when the palace site was reoccupied.

The west wing

From the south propylaea the visitor ascends a wide **staircase (7)** to the restored first floor of the western wing (the piano nobile, according to A. Evans). The partly roofed, today, ground floor of the west wing includes the MAGAZINES **(B)**, the THRONE ROOM complex **(C)**, and the complex of the CENTRAL SHRINE **(D)**.

To the east of the great staircase is a **rectangular structure (17)** which Arthur Evans initially thought to be a "Mycenean palace" and later a "Greek" temple dedicated to the goddess Rhea, which seems to be the more plausible theory.

On the first floor there were great ceremonial rooms with colonnades, which have been given conventional names (**Shrine Room, Great Hall,** etc.) **(8)**. These rooms were adorned with beautiful frescoes, among which the famous fresco of the "Offerings", the "Parisienne", the miniature of the three-columned shrine.

From the restored roof of the western wing one can see the eighteen large WESTERN MAGAZINES, which extend over the entire western half of the wing. The magazines are oblong rooms which have openings to the west towards the long and wide **paved corridor (9)**. The large pithoi are lined up along two rows, while between them there are rows of deep square pits whose sides are faced with gypsum slabs, and which served as storage containers for liquids. The jars themselves were used mainly to store dry supplies. There were jars and storage compartments in the corridor, too. The magazines and the corridor provided space for a total of 400 jars, although only 150 were actually found there. They had an estimated total capacity of 80,000 litres. Various symbols were inscribed on the walls of the magazines: double axes, stars, branches, which indicate the sacred nature of these rooms. Signs of the fire which destroyed the palace are still visible in various parts of the magazines.

In a covered room above the Throne Room some reproductions of frescoes from

The western magazines with pithoi

various parts of the palace are on display: the fresco of the "festivities before the shrine" and of the "dance in the sacred wood", the frescoes of the "Ladies in Blue", of the bull-leaping, of the "Argonaut", of the "Blue Monkey", the "Blue Bird", and the "Captain of the Blacks". From this room a small set of steps brings one down to the antechamber of the throne room.

From the first floor of the west wing, the visitor descends by the grand double-colonnaded **west stairway (10)** to the paved CENTRAL COURT **(E)**, a large, rectangular area. Anyone wishing to pass from one wing of the palace to the other passed through the central court, which

**Restored staircase
to the second floor**

served as a light well and an air shaft for the palace which towered, many-storeyed, around it. It seems probable that in the central court various festivities and ceremonies took place. This is where the northern and southern entrance led into. Its paved floor has only survived in the northwestern and southwestern corners. Its pavement slabs, together with enormous quantities of other building stones of the palace were transported to Candia and used in the construction of its defence wall during the period of Venetian rule. In the lower strata of the court, the

successive phases of the Neolithic settlement were excavated and studied.

From the central court, the visitor can see the THRONE ROOM complex **(C)**, which dates, in the form in which it has survived, from the fourth phase of the new palace, the so-called "Mycenean" phase. Two steps down, and through the polythyron (a complex of openings), the visitor first comes into the **antechamber (11)**, which has a gypsum bench on the north and south sides, and a low base, where stood a wooden throne. In the middle of the antechamber there is a basin made of porphyry. Here, during the excavations, were found the squat "alabastra" (perfume bottles or ointment vases) which were hastily abandoned when disaster struck

the palace. Access to the **main hall (12)** is through a double entrance. Here we find the gypsum throne in the centre of the north wall, and benches on the north, west and south sides. There is also a **"lustral basin" (13)** on the south side. To the right and left of the throne there are reproductions of the fresco with the griffins. These imaginary creatures, with the head of an eagle and body of a lion, symbolize royal and divine power. This room had a religious function, and Evans believed that it was perhaps here that Minos met with the priesthood, who were also charged with the administration of justice. It is for this reason that a wooden copy of the throne was made in the Hague, for the president of the International

**The antechamber
to the throne room**

Court of Justice, which has its seat in that city of the Netherlands. To the west and north of the room there are closed areas, with built ledges for the idols of the goddess and for other cult objects and vessels.

South of the throne room complex we find the complex of the CENTRAL SHRINE **(D)**, immediately south of the western staircase. Here is the **tripartite shrine (14),** whose facade is familiar to us from the fresco of the same name, and the **temple repositories (15)** consisting of square built pits, where the famous snake goddesses and other ritual objects of the shrine

53

The central tripartite shrine

The throne room complex

The throne room

The fresco of the "Parisienne"

The miniature fresco
of the tripartite shrine

shrine were kept. To the west there are two rooms with central square pillars. The square pillars are inscribed with sacred symbols and in front and behind them there are small stone basins for liquid offerings. This, then, is where some kind of pillar worship took place, as the divinity was believed to inhabit them.

If we cross the central court to the south, we come to its southern side, where the last portion of the **processional way (18)** has been restored. On the wall, a reproduction of the relief fresco has been placed. It is known as the fresco of the "Priest King (or Prince)", and he is portrayed surrounded by lilies and leading a griffin or a sphinx by a rope which he is holding in his hand.

Recently, it has been claimed that the pieces of the fresco represent three figures, two boxers and a priestess, wearing a magnificent crown.

**A faience statuette:
the snake godess**

**The miniature fresco
of the tripartite shrine**

EAST WING

In the middle of the central court, we find the **grand staircase (19)**, from where the visit of the eastern wing of the palace begins. This is where we will find the ROYAL APARTMENTS (**F**), the HALL OF THE DOUBLE AXES (**G**), the EAST HALL (**I**), and the AREA OF THE WORKSHOPS (**H**). The ruins in this part of the palace were found in relatively good condition, because the walls survived to a fair height, thanks to the fact that the structure was built into a cutting of a slope, eight metres below the level of the central court. This allowed the palace to be built to a height of five storeys (the ground floor being level with the bottom of the cutting and four floors above it) while, in the west wing, it was three storeys high (one at the level of the court and two above it). The ground floor and the upper floors of the "royal apartments" were linked by

59

The grand staircase

means of a monumental system of stairways, known as the grand staircase. The grand staircase with the gypsum steps is one of the wonders of Minoan architecture. It consists of two wings of staircases, repeated at each floor level. It is lit by a large light well situated to the east, and is surrounded by colonnades which create successive balconies. Four flights have been preserved: the two upper ones have been restored and the two lower ones are as they were found. The great width of the stairway, the low tread and slight slant of the steps, facilitating ascent or descent, are worthy of notice. The balcony of the guards owes its name to the great figure-of-eight shields which were painted on its

walls (a reproduction here).

Having taken the stairs down to the ground level and followed the corridor to the east, the visitor comes to the king's megaron, also known as **Hall of the Double Axes (21)**, which has been given this name from this sacred symbol which has been incised on the blocks of the walls around. The megaron consists of the main hall with the polythyra and porticoes to the west, east and south which look onto light wells. In the western portico were found the ruins of a stately throne, which had been buried under a great block of porous limestone. The throne was a wooden one and was surrounded by small columns which held up a canopy. Today it is protected by a glass case. The polythyra were closed by double doors, which could be drawn inside the jambs, thus creating a single space where a large number of people could assemble, and also creating a

The balcony with the shields

draught to cool the room. A wooden throne may perhaps have stood against the north wall. The walls of the megaron, of the upper floor and of the verandah were adorned with frescoes of figure-of-eight shields, of an Argonaut, of a bull, which have partially survived. They date from the period of the "Mycenean palace" of the fourth phase.

From the "King's Megaron" the visitor follows a corridor and reaches the **"Queen's Megaron" (22)**, which is slightly smaller but sumptuously built, with multiple windows and benches, a portico and a light well and with auxiliary areas: a bathroom with a clay tub, a toilet and a dressing room. A small shrine on the floor above the megaron was a wonderful treasure trove which yielded a number of small objects:

The portico of the king's megaron

an ivory acrobat or "taurokathaptis" and other ivory pieces depicting various figures and a bull, a tiny golden fish etc. Here, too, was found the gold and ivory "Boston goddess" (considered by some scholars to be a fake) which was unearthed before the excavations began, and was illegally smuggled out of the country. The "Queen's Megaron" was adorned with marvellous frescoes (of dolphins, dancers, spirals etc.). Between the two megara and around them there were stairways linking the various rooms and floors. A system of light wells provided light and air.

In the southern part of the eastern wing we find the **"Shrine of the Double Axes" (G)**, a complex which dates - in the form we see it today - from the "Mycenean

The queen's bathroom

**The restored upper storey
of the king's megaron**

**The king's megaron from
the southeast**

phase" of the palace. Here there is a
bench-altar (23), where the idols of the
divinity and other cult objects were placed.
There is also a "lustral basin", while stone,
pyramid-shaped bases for double axes were
found here, as well.

From the Shrine of the Double Axes the
visitor must return to the outside corridors
of the megara and from there continue his
tour in the area of the PALACE WORK-
SHOPS **(8)**. The **lapidary's workshop
(25)** stood here, and the lumps of Spartan
basalt on which he was working can still be

seen, as he left them when disaster struck.
Next to it is the **potter's workshop (26)**,
with a low bench and a plaster basin for
moulding the clay. A room above the
potter's work-shop was adorned with the
fresco of the "Taurokathapsia" (toreador
fresco). North of the workshop is the court
of the **"Stone Spout" (27)**. To the east is
the stepped **eastern entrance (29)**, with
a system for the drainage of rain-water
consisting of conduits running down the
sides of the steps and drainage wells at
intervals.

North of the narrow modern stairway are
the **Magazines of the Giant Pithoi
(28)**, which belong to the period of the old
palace. Further north were the potters'

**The fresco
of the dolphins**

**The queen's
megaron**

Detail from the Shrine
of the Double Axes

The workshop
area

The lapidary's
workshop

Façades of buildings and a tree on faience plaques

The fresco of the ladies

workshops and the **Northeastern magazines (34)** of the old palace.

Taking the small modern stairway to the west, the visitor climbs to the site of the large EASTERN HALL **(I)**, the ground floor of which has now been restored and covered. This was the **Magazine of the Medallion Pithoi (30).**

The fresco of the "Ladies in Blue" was found in this area. In one of the small rooms was also found the famous "Town Mosaic", consisting of faience plaques representing the facades of Minoan houses. All these finds come from the storey where the large hall is situated. Here, too, is the **Corridor of the Bays (32).**

The great eastern hall is thought to have been the formal throne room. In this hall stood the colossal *xoanon* (wooden cult statue) of the great goddess, of which only the bronze plaits of hair have been preserved. Charred masses of wood were found during the excavations on the northern side of the hall. The height of the statue is estimated to have been 2.80 m. The walls of the hall were adorned with the magnificent reliefs depicting scenes of athletic contests and griffins tied to pillars.

North of the great hall there are various areas, such as the **"Corridor of the Draughtboard" (33)**, where the famous royal gaming table which resembles a chessboard was found. Sections of the drainage system have also been preserved and can be seen here. Other areas have also been given conventional names: the Northeast Hall, the Eastern Magazines, the Olive Press etc. The area with the partitions perhaps served as kennels or stables for the palace animals.

Passing along the northeastern magazines, the visitor finds himself in the complex of the NORTH ENTRANCE **(J)**, where there is the large northern pillared hall, known as the **"Customs House" (36)**. This large hall had three aisles with eight square

71

The Corridor of the Bays

pillars holding up the roof. This is where the harbour road ended, and archaeologists have conjectured that this is where the goods unloaded from the ships were brought. It is also possible that it may have served as a banquet hall. From the Customs house begins th**e ramp of the North Entrance (37)** leading to the Central Court. On either side of the ramp there were imposing balconies. One of the balconies (bastion) has been restored; in the colonnade above it a reproduction of the relief fresco of the Charging Bull can be seen.

The last section of the palace which must be visited is the NORTHWESTERN SECTION **(K)** - or "northwest insula" according to Evans. Here there are six very deep **basement rooms (39)**, which are enclosed by a rectangular wall. Evans

Relief fresco of a seated woman

The northeastern area

called these rooms "cells", but they could have been storerooms. They belong to the old palace. Above the "cells", during the period of the new palace, a shrine with a paved floor and a square pillar in the centre was built. The upper part was adorned with frescoes. Here were found the fragments of miniature frescoes of the Tripartite Shrine, of the Sacred Wood and of the Saffron-Gatherer. One of the rooms of this area contained a large number of tablets with inscriptions in Linear B script. North of this area is the restored northern **"Lustral basin" (38)**.

As he leaves the palace, on the western side, the visitor comes to the famous and unique THEATRE **(L)** of Knossos. The theatre was one of the ceremonial areas of the palace and of the city of Knossos. The seats have been arranged in two inter-

The medallion pithoi

The inscribed plaques in Linear A and Linear B scripts

The northern area

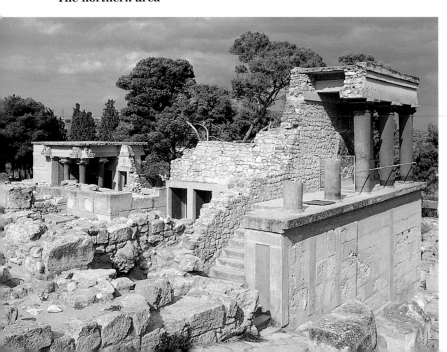

The relief fresco of the bull

The balcony with the
relief fresco of the bull

The customs house and
the north entrance

The theatre

The northern lustral basin

secting "wings" **(40)**, the east and the south wing. At the point where the two wings meet, was the "royal box". The theatre is thought to have been able to accommodate 400 spectators. This is where the famous paved ROYAL ROAD with the **processional corridor (41)** ended. It led to the little palace, after passing through the city. Some of the larger and more important houses of the city stood along the royal road (House of the Frescoes etc.) From the theatre, the visitor returns to the west court, and from there to the exit of the archaeological site.

THE HOUSES AROUND THE PALACE

Some of the most interesting excavated

The royal road

houses of the city are to be found within the fenced-in main archaeological site and can be visited. In relation to the palace, the "House of the Frescoes" is to the northwest, the "South House", as its name indicates, to the south, and to the southeast the "House of the Fallen Blocks", the "House of the Sacrificed Oxen", the "House of the High Priest (or of the Chancel Screen)" and the "Southeast House".

The **"House of the Frescoes" (42)** is situated south of the royal road and owes its name to the stack of fragmented frescoes found in one of its rooms. These

79

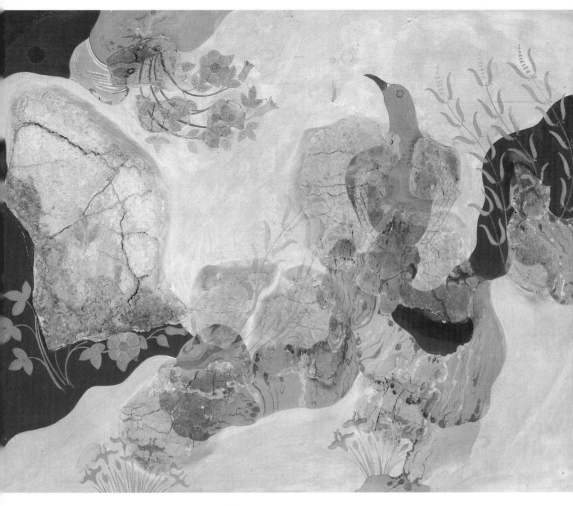

The fresco of the blue bird

The fresco of the blue monkey

frescoes are among the most famous of Knossos: the "Blue Bird" fresco, the "Blue Monkey", the "Gardens", the "Captain of the Blacks". Reproductions of these frescoes are now in the room above the Throne Room in the palace.

The **"South House "** (43) is situated at a lower level than the palace, below its southwestern corner. It was built beside the stepped portico during the second neopalatial period, when that portico fell into disuse. It was a three-storey structure and was restored by Sir Arthur Evans. Recently, new work has begun to strengthen the structure. It has some very interesting architectural elements: a pillar crypt, a lustral basin, a stand for a double axe. Among the finds in this house, worth mentioning is the discovery of a hoard of silver vessels and another one of bronze tools.

The **"House of the Sacrificed Oxen"** (45) and the **"House of the Fallen Blocks"** (44) date from the first neopalatial period. Their names are due to the discovery, in the former, of remains of a sacrifice (a tripod altar and horns of a bull) and in the latter, to the blocks of stone which were hurled down into the house by the earthquake from the facade of the palace. The **"House of the High Priest"** or the **"House of the Chancel Screen"** (4) has a dais and a partition with two columns. The **"Southeast House"** (46) was well built and adorned with frescoes of lilies. It has a polythyron, a pillared crypt and a stand for a double axe. Here, a beautiful lamp of porphyry was also found. Further to the north there are ruins of houses of the old palace period.

Here ends the visit of the fenced-in area of the palace.The remainder of the houses and monuments are situated outside it.

THE "LITTLE PALACE" (M) AND THE "UNEXPLORED MANSION"

These are to the west of the tarred road, before the entrance to the modern settle-

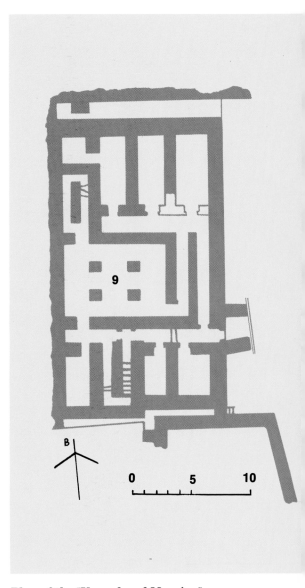

Plan of the "Unexplored Mansion"

ment. The **Little Palace** covers approximately 1500 sq. metres and is lavishly built, with all the architectural elements which are to be found in the great palace. Its entrance (1) to the east led to stately reception areas: the Entrance Hall (2), the Hall of the Peristyle (3), a double Megaron with polythyra (4) and a portico to the east. It also had a "lustral basin", which was transformed, during the postpalatial

81

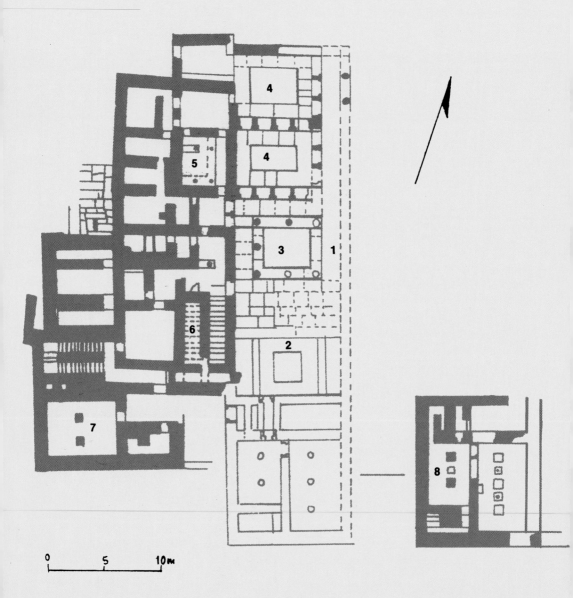

1. Entrance
2. Entrance hall
3. Colonnaded hall
4. Megaron
5. Shrine
6. Staircase
7.-8. Crypts

period, into a shrine of "fetish" figures (5). A grand staircase led to the first floor. There were also pillar crypts on the ground floor beneath the entrance (8) and in the southwestern corner (7). In a repository near the southwestern crypt was found the magnificent steatite rhyton in the shape of a bull's head now in the Herakleion Museum.

A paved way and a small flagstoned court to the west separates the "Little Palace" from the **"Unexplored Mansion" (9)**, which was excavated about twenty years ago, and of which only the impressive western facade was known to us. This mansion was linked to the Little Palace by a bridge. It was built during the second neopalatial period and was used again during the "Mycenean phase" and thereafter. It is rectangular in shape and was built with skilfully hewn blocks of stone. It has a central hall with four square pillars, corridors, magazines and a stairway to the upper floor.

THE "ROYAL VILLA" (N), THE "GUEST HOUSE" AND THE "SACRED SPRING" (O)

The **Royal Villa (N)** is situated to the northeast of the palace, south of the settlement of Makrys Toichos. It is built into a cutting in the side of the hill and overlooks the Kairatos valley. Its construction is luxurious and has been carried out with meticulous care. The entrance is through an anteroom (1), into the Megaron with its row of three doors (polythyra) (2), where there is a semicircular recess on the west side for the throne (3) and columns on a partition. It also has a pillar crypt with a square pillar (4) and in the floor there are small stone basins to catch the liquid offerings. A double stairway (5) led to the upper floor, where the entrance to the Villa was perhaps situated.

The **Guest house (O)** is situated to the south, opposite the palace, to which it is linked by the viaduct. It was thought to have been used for receiving guests coming to Knossos from the south. In a room which has been restored today, the famous fresco with the partridges was found. (A copy has been set in its place). The other room was a bathroom.

West of the Guest House (or Caravanserai) complex was the Spring Chamber, where the waters of the Vlychia spring welled up until only recently. The room has ledges for offerings and a niche for a lamp. We have here an interesting example of a **"spring shrine"**.

THE SOUTH ROYAL TEMPLE TOMB (P)

This is the southernmost monument of Minoan Knossos and is situated at a distance of approximately 600 metres from the palace. Its construction is perfect, with dressed blocks of poros - a royal edifice indeed. It combines the function of tomb and shrine and is a unique monument of prehistoric Greece. It was excavated following the chance discovery here of a golden ring, the famous ring of Minos, which has today been lost. The temple tomb consists of an entrance, through a court with a portico, a small antechamber, a pillar crypt with two square pillars and a rock-cut burial chamber with walls lined with gypsum slabs, and a square gypsum pillars in the middle. The finds date one of the last burials in the main burial chamber, to the Mycenean phase of Knossos. Sir Arthur Evans believed that this is where the last Minos was buried. A stairway leads to the upper floor of the monument, which had columns and was surmounted by double horns of consecration.

This tomb greatly resembles the tomb described by Diodorus as having been built for Minos in Sicily and which consisted of a tomb below and a shrine above.

To the west and north of the royal tomb, at Gypsades, are the so-called **"Hogarth's Houses" (Q)**. These were large and important mansions which were named after the British archaeologist who excavated them in the early years of this

Plan of the little palace

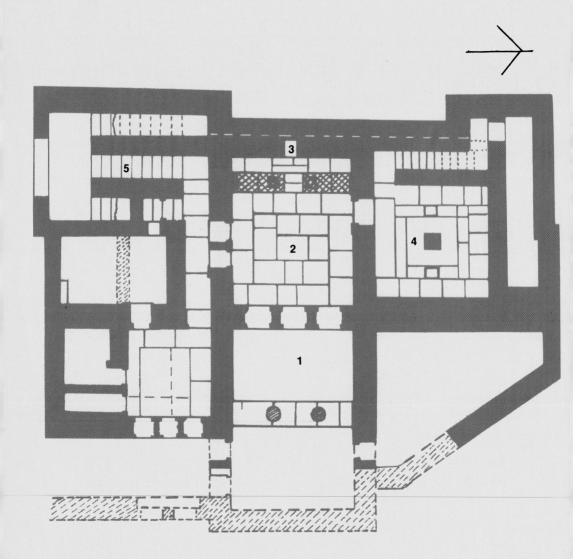

1. Antechamber
2. Megaron
3. Recess
4. Crypt
5. Staircase

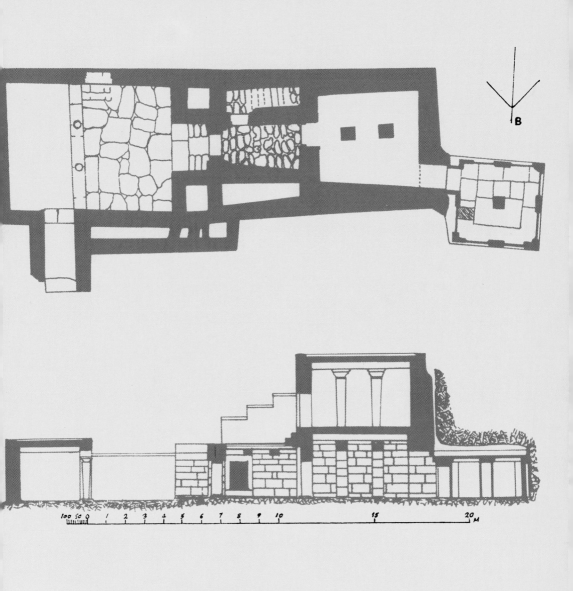

The southern royal tomb

Plan of the royal villa

The fresco of the partridges

**Piece of gold jewellery from the
tomb of Tekés**

century

Another royal tomb in Knossos and also quite unique, was the famous **TOMB OF THE ISOPATA**, situated at a distance of 2.5 kilometres to the north of the palace. This tomb had a rock-cut dromos, a built antechamber and an oblong burial chamber roofed by a stone vault. Unfortunately this unique monument was destroyed by the Germans during the war and its material used for the construction of a pill-box.

Depiction of a ritual dance on the gold ring of Isopata

Marble statue of the god Dionysus

THE VILLA DIONYSUS (R)

The Villa Dionysus is one of the monuments of the post- Minoan period which can be visited. It dates from the Roman period (2nd century AD, during the time of the emperor Hadrian). The villa is situated in the enclosed area of the Villa Ariadne, 250 metres to the north. It owes its name to its unique mosaic floors which portray the god Dionysus. It consists of a peristyle in the middle, with Doric columns of poros stone. To the west is the "oikos", and to the north and south other rooms, all of them with mosaic floors decorated with geometric patterns and Dionysiac scenes. Here was found the statue of the emperor Hadrian which is now in the Archaeological Museum of Heraklion.

THE MAUSOLEUM ON THE UNIVERSITY GROUNDS (S)

The only mausoleum to have been preserved, in the area north of the University, dates from the same period. It is an underground burial monument of dressed poros. It has a descending stairway, a low entrance with monolithic jambs and lintel, and a rectangular chamber with three monolithic funerary beds standing on stone legs. The tomb was roofed with a barrel vault of hewn stone. The finds date the tomb to the period between the 2nd to the 4th century AD. It was destroyed by an earthquake in 365 AD.

EPILOGUE

Here ends our visit to Knossos. We hope the visitor to the ruins of this unique Minoan palace and city has formed a vivid picture of this splendid first Hellenic civilization. However, this picture would not be complete without a visit to the Archaeological Museum of Herakleion, where the treasures from the excavations at Knossos are exhibited.

Marble statue of the Emperor Hadrian

Reconstruction of the palace (according to C. Iliakis)

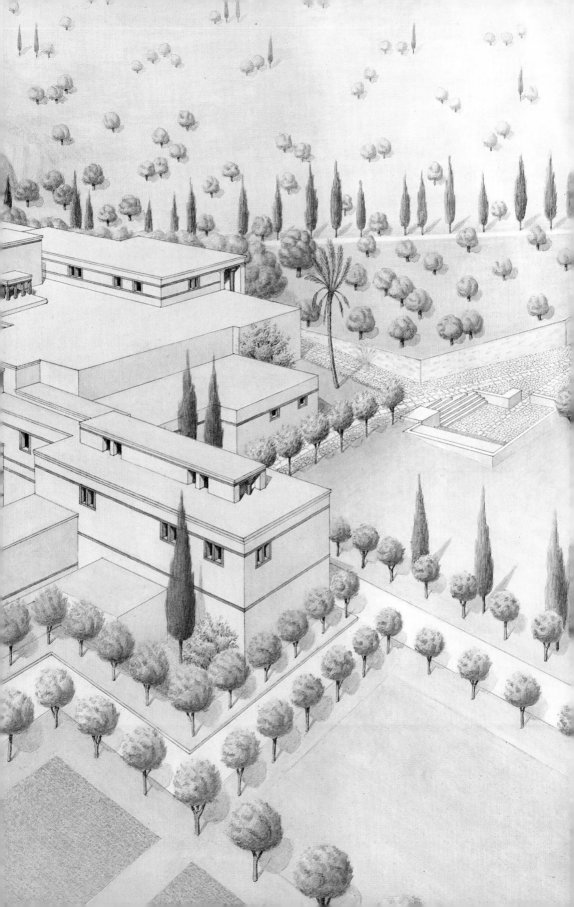

BIBLIOGRAPHY

Alexiou, St., *Μινωϊκός πολιτισμός, με οδηγό των ανακτόρων: Ανάκτορον Κνωσού*, 131-196 (Ηράκλειο 1964)

Brock J.,*Fortezza: Early Greek Tombs near Knossos* (Cambrige 1957)

Brown A., *Arthur Evans and the Palace of Minos* (Oxford 1983)

Cadogan G., *The palaces of Minoan Crete: Knossos* 50-91, (London and New York 1976

Cadogan G., *"Knossos" in the Aerial Atlas of Ancient Crete* (eds. J. W. Myers - E. E. Myers - G. Cadogan, Berkeley 1992), 127-147

Coldstream J.N., *Knossos: The Sanctuary of Demeter* (London 1973)

Evans A. J., Knossos: *The Palace of Minos at Knossos*, vols. I-IV (London 1921-1935)

Evans J., *Neolithic Knossos: The Growth of a Settlement, Proceedings of the Prehistoric Society* (1971), 95-117.

Graham W.J., *The Palaces of Crete: Knossos*, 23-33, 51-58 and passim (Princeton 1972

Hood M.S., *The Minoans*, 65-72 and passim (London 1971)

The Bronze Age Palace at Knossos (Plan and Sections) (London 1981)

Archaeological Survey of the Knossos Area (London 1981)

Hutchinson, R., *Prehistoric Crete, Knossos*:170-81, 270-9 and passim (Harmondsworth 1962)

Kalokairinos M., *Ανασκαφές στην Κνωσό*, Παλίμψηστον 9/10, παράρτημα, 5-69 (ed. Κ. Κόπακα)

Krontira L. - Vasilakis A., *Πρώτη Γνωριμία με την Κρήτη του Μίνωα* (Athens 1988)

Michailidis A., *Knossos, A Complete Guide to the Palace of Minos*

Pendlebury J., *A Handbook to the Palace of Minos, Knossos* (London 1954) and in the Greek translation by Nikolaos Platon: *Οδηγός Κνωσσού* (Herakleion 1950)

The Archaeology of Crete, Knossos: passim (London 1939)

Platon N., *Ιστορία του Ελληνικού Εθνους Α: Κνωσός*, 170-9 (Athens 1970)

Popham M., *Minoan Unexplored Mansion* (London 1984)

Powell D., *The Villa Ariadne* (London 1973)

Sakellarakis G. and E., *Κρήτη: Ιστορία και Πολιτισμός: Νεολιθική και Μινωϊκή Κρήτη*, 3-130 (Ηράκλειο 1987)

Sanders I., *Roman Crete*, 51-3, 67-70, 105-7, 152-3 and passim (Wilts 1982)

Vasilakis A., *Μινωϊκή Κρήτη, με οδηγό των αρχαιολογικών χώρων: Κνωσός*, 178-190 (Ηράκλειο 1992)

Ventris M. - Chadwick J., *Documents in Mycenean Greek* (Cambridge 1956)

Zois A., *Κρήτη, Εποχή του Λίθου: Κνωσός* 133-174 (Athens 1973)

INDEXES

Modern

Abbreviations:
EMI: Early Minoan I
MMI: Middle Minoan I
LMI: Late Minoan I
Dating of periods according to Evans

Phototypesetting: Argyris Vavouris
Montage: Pergamos S.A.
Printed by: Pergamos S.A